colorwork stitches

THE HARMONY GUIDES

colorwork stitches

over 250 designs to knit

edited by Susie Johns

INTERWEAVE.
interweavebooks.com

First published in the United States by
Interweave Press LLC
201 East Fourth Street
Loveland, CO 80537-5655
Interweavebooks.com

Picture credits:
2, 5, 7 Michael Wicks
6, 9 top row left and right, second row center, third row left Corbis
9 third row right, bottom row center Istock
All other photography by Geoff Dann
Illustrations by Lotte Oldfield

10 9 8 7 6 5 4 3 2 1

Reproduction by Dot Gradations Ltd, UK
Printed and bound by 1010 Printing International Ltd, China

contents

inspiration

Color is the inspiration for this edition: two or more different colored yarns cleverly combined to produce a multitude of patterns, each presented as a clear, easy-to follow chart and a knitted stitch sample.

For more than 30 years, The Harmony Guides have provided a unique reference for knitters, providing a wealth of stitch information and inspiration for everyone who likes to knit, regardless of their skill level.

This new generation of Harmony Guides contains not only traditional patterns but new and innovative ones too. Browse through the pages and you will find simple motifs, more intricate patterns and some really challenging designs ready for you to select, combine and incorporate into your knitting projects. Whether you are making a scarf or hat, a sweater or jacket, a cushion cover or a blanket, you will find stitch patterns to bring color and visual interest into your project.

Fair Isle knitting uses design repeats and motifs in horizontal and vertical bands, and in small and large panels. Typically, Fair Isle patterns feature diagonal lines which means that the color-change positions are offset, creating an elastic fabric; and no more than two colors are used in any row, one color being "stranded" across the back of the other. There is also a symmetry to the patterns, which means they can easily be memorized.

Intarsia knitting is a similar technique, though yarn is usually not stranded across the back of the work and patterns often involve larger blocks of color and picture motifs.

Most of the designs in this book draw their inspiration from traditional Scottish and Scandinavian patterns and can be combined in all kinds of ways. Traditional Fair Isle designs are usually made up of horizontal bands of patterning. The bands can vary from a single row to 30 or more rows and can be combined with panels and with all-over designs.

Of course, the modern knitter does not have to follow any rules and you can be as creative as you like. A good starting point is to draw your design on graph paper using colored pencils or pens, or to use a computer program that allows you to create a grid and fill it in with blocks of color. It also helps to knit swatches, to see how a chosen pattern can change dramatically when various different color combinations are used, such as changing a background color from dark to light, by using contrasting or clashing colors, or by using different shades and tones of one color.

Fine yarns are favored by traditionalists—like me—when knitting Fair Isle patterns. I like to use a two-ply jumper-weight Shetland yarn, combining solid-colored dyed yarns with natural undyed yarns and with tweedy, flecked yarns for subtle color changes. These patterns can, however, be knitted using yarns of any weight. The choice is yours.

If the idea of knitting a whole garment in a color pattern seems too daunting, why not incorporate a patterned border into something that is otherwise plain? You could add a wave border to either end of a scarf, for example, or all round the hem of a knitted skirt or jacket. A sweater or cardigan could feature a Fair Isle band, a patterned medallion on a pocket or a scattering of small motifs. A child's sweater could have a row of Lads and Lasses dancing across the front or a single intarsia motif, while a baby's cradle cover could have flowers or bows all round the edges.

Pillow covers are a blank canvas for all kinds of color work. You could add a small color motif to an otherwise plain panel, large or small; combine a selection of patterns for an all-over design; or save your experimental swatches and gauge squares and stitch them all together to make a patchwork blanket.

If you don't have the patience for a big project, think of all the small items you could make using any of the patterns in this book. Knit a single border pattern in your own choice of colors and add elastic to make a headband, a buckle to create a belt, or use it as the strap for a shoulder bag. Work patterned strips in the round to make tubes of knitted fabric that can be worn as cuffs or legwarmers, or which can be stuffed with wadding to make a funky draught excluder. Stitch two small swatches together and you have a slipcase for your MP3 player, digital camera or passport, or make larger pieces to create a knitted portable computer case.

If you are new to color knitting and you find you become hooked, pass on your new-found skills to someone else. Then get together with friends or family members and create individual squares that can be joined to make a quilt or picnic blanket—perhaps one that uses every single pattern in the book!

Best of all, be happy in the knowledge that you are helping to continue—and in some cases even revive—a centuries-old knitting tradition.

Susie Johns

tools & equipment

To master any skill, it's imperative to have a solid foundation of the techniques. This section provides useful information that can come in handy while knitting.

Knitting Needles

Knitting needles are used in pairs to produce a flat knitted fabric. They are pointed at one end to form the stitches and have a knob at the other to retain the stitches. They may be made in plastic, wood, steel, or alloy and range in size from 2mm to 17mm in diameter. In the UK, needles used to be sized by numbers—the higher the number, the smaller the needle. In the USA, the opposite is true—higher numbers indicate larger sizes. Metric sizing has now been internationally adopted. Needles are also made in different lengths that will comfortably hold the number of stitches required for each project.

It is useful to have a range of sizes available so that gauge swatches can be knitted up and compared. Discard any needles that become bent. Points should be fairly sharp; blunt needles reduce the speed and ease of working.

Circular and double-pointed needles are used to produce a tubular fabric or flat rounds. Many traditional fishermen's sweaters are knitted in the round. Double-pointed needles

are sold in sets of four or five. Circular needles consist of two needles joined by a flexible length of plastic. The plastic varies in length. Use the shorter lengths for knitting sleeves, neckbands, etc, and the longer lengths for larger pieces such as sweaters and skirts.

Cable needles are short needles used to hold the stitches of a cable to the back or front of the main body of knitting.

Other Useful Equipment

Needle gauges are punched with holes corresponding to the needle sizes and are marked with both the old numerical sizing and the metric sizing so you can easily check the size of any needle.

Stitch holders resemble large safety pins and are used to hold stitches while they are not being worked—for example, around a neckline when the neckband stitches will be picked up and worked after back and front have been joined. As an alternative, thread a larger blunt-pointed sewing needle with a generous length of contrast-colored yarn, thread it through the stitches to be held while they are still on the needle, then slip the stitches off the needle and knot both ends of the contrast yarn to secure the stitches.

Wool sewing needles or tapestry needles are used to sew completed pieces of knitting together. They are large with a broad eye for easy threading and a blunt point that will slip between the knitted stitches without splitting and fraying the yarn. Do not use the sharp-pointed sewing needles to sew up knitting.

A row counter is used to count the number of rows that have been knitted. It is a cylinder with a numbered dial that is pushed onto the needle and the dial is turned at the completion of each row.

A tape measure is essential for measuring the length and width of completed knitting. For checking gauge swatches, it is better to use a rigid ruler. For an accurate result, always smooth the knitting (without stretching) on a firm flat surface before measuring it.

A crochet hook is useful for picking up dropped stitches.

Knitting Yarn

Yarn is the term used for strands of spun fibers that are twisted together into a continuous length of the required thickness. Yarn can be of animal origin (wool, angora, mohair, silk, alpaca), vegetable origin (cotton, linen), or man-made (nylon, acrylic, rayon). Knitting yarn may be made up from a combination of two or more different fibers.

Each single strand of yarn is known as a ply. A number of plys are twisted together to form the yarn. The texture and characteristics of the yarn may be varied by the combination of fibers and by the way in which the yarn is spun. Wool and other natural fibers are often combined with man-made fibers to make a yarn that is more economical and hard-wearing. Wool can also be treated to make it machine washable. If the twist of the yarn is firm and smooth, it knits up into a hard-wearing fabric. Loosely twisted yarn has a softer finish when knitted.

Buying Yarn

Yarn is most commonly sold wound into balls of specific weight measured into grams or ounces. Some yarn, particularly very thick yarn, is also sold in a coiled hank or skein that must be wound into a ball before you can begin knitting.

Yarn manufacturers (called spinners) wrap each ball with a paper band on which is printed a lot of necessary information. The ball band states the weight of the yarn and its composition. It will give instructions for washing and ironing and will state the ideal range of needle sizes to be used with the yarn. The ball band also carries the shade number and dye lot number. It is important that you use yarn of the same dye lot for an entire project. Different dye lots vary subtly and this may not be apparent when you are holding the two balls, but it may show as a variation in shade on the finished piece of knitting.

Always keep the ball band as a reference. The best way is to pin it to the gauge swatch (see page 20) and keep them together with any left over yarn and spare buttons or other trimmings. That way you can always check the washing instructions and also have materials for repairs.

the basics

Once you have mastered the basics of knitting, you can go on to develop your skills and start making more challenging projects.

Casting On

1 Make a slip knot 39in (1m) from the end of the yarn. Hold the needle in your right hand with the ball end of the yarn over your index finger. Wind the loose end of the yarn around your left thumb from front to back.

2 Insert the point of the needle under the first strand of yarn on your thumb.

3 With your right index finger, take the ball end of the yarn over the point of the needle.

4 Pull a loop through to form the first stitch. Remove your left thumb from the yarn. Pull the loose end to secure the stitch. Repeat until all stitches have been cast on.

Knit Stitch

1 Hold the needle with the cast-on stitches in your left hand, with the loose yarn at the back of the work. Insert the right-hand needle from front to back of the first stitch on the left-hand needle.

2 Wind the yarn from left to right over the point of the right-hand needle.

3 Draw the yarn through the stitch, thus forming a new stitch on the right-hand needle.

4 Slip the original stitch off the left-hand needle, keeping the new stitch on the right-hand needle.

5 To knit a row, repeat steps 1 to 4 until all the stitches have been transferred from the left-hand needle to the right-hand needle. Turn the work, transferring the needle with the stitches to your left hand to work the next row.

Purl Stitch

I Hold the needle with the stitches in your left hand with the loose yarn at the front of the work. Insert the right-hand needle from back to front of the first stitch on the left-hand needle.

2 Wind the yarn from right to left over the point of the right-hand needle.

3 Draw the yarn through the stitch, thus forming a new stitch on the right-hand needle.

4 Slip the original stitch off the left-hand needle, keeping the new stitch on the right-hand needle.

5 To purl a row, repeat steps 1 to 4 until all the stitches have been transferred from the left-hand needle to the right-hand needle. Turn the work, transferring the needle with the stitches to your left hand to work the next row.

Increasing

The simplest method of increasing one stitch is to work into the front and back of the same stitch.

On a knit row, knit into the front of the stitch to be increased, then before slipping it off the needle, place the right-hand needle behind the left-hand needle and knit again into the back of the same stitch. Slip the original stitch off the left-hand needle.

On a purl row, purl into the front of the stitch to be increased, then before slipping it off the needle, purl again into the back of the same stitch. Slip the original stitch off the left-hand needle.

Decreasing

The simplest method of decreasing one stitch is to work two stitches together.

On a knit row, insert the right-hand needle from front to back through two stitches instead of one, then knit them together as one stitch. This is called knit two together (k2tog).

On a purl row, insert the right-hand needle from back to front through two stitches instead of one, then purl them together as one stitch. This is called purl two together (p2tog).

Joining in a new color on a knit row

When working Fair Isle, it is better to join in a new color at the beginning of a row, but in some cases, you may have to join in the middle of a row. This is how you join in a new color mid-row on a knit row.

1 Lay the new color (B) over the original color (A). Twist the yarns over themselves and hold them in place.

2 Knit with the new color (B). You can always go back and tighten the join after a couple of stitches.

Joining in a new color on a purl row

This is how you join in a new color mid-row on a purl row.

1 Lay the new color (B) over the original color (A). Twist the yarns over themselves and hold them in place.

2 Purl with the new color (B).

Joining in a new color in the middle of a row

When working in intarsia you will find yourself needing to join in a new color in the middle of a row.

1 On a knit row, knit to the change in color. Lay the new color over the existing color and between the two needles, with the tail to the left.

2 Bring the new color under and then over the existing color.

3 Knit the stitch with the new color. Go back and pull gently on the tail to tighten up the first stitch in the new color after you have knitted a couple more stitches.

Changing colors in a straight vertical line

Once you have joined in a new color you may need to work for a number of rows changing these colors on both the knit rows and purl rows. This is often confusingly referred to as "twisting" the yarns but it is a link rather than a twist. It is a common mistake to over-twist the yarns at this point and then the fabric will not lie flat.

1 On a knit row, knit to the change in color. Bring the new color up from under the old color and drop the old color so that the new color is ready to work with.

2 On a purl row, knit to the change in color. Bring the new color from the left under the old color and up to the top. Drop the old color and continue with the new color.

Eliminating ends

If you are working a complex design it is always best to look for ways of eliminating ends so that you can cut down the number of hours that will be needed to sew them all in.

Look for shapes that perhaps have an outline, as with this diamond motif.

I Take a length of the yarn required to work the whole motif and fold it in half. On the center stitch of the motif, loop the fold over the right-hand needle.

2 On the next row, take one end of the yarn to the right and the other to the left, linking the outline and background colors on each row. If the motif is very small and the background color remains the same, it is best to carry the background color across the back of the motif, weaving it in if necessary.

Binding Off

There is one simple, most commonly used method of securing stitches once you have finished a piece of knitting —binding off. The bind-off edge should always have the same "give" or elasticity as the fabric and you should always bind off in the stitch pattern used for the main fabric unless the pattern directs otherwise.

Knitwise

Knit two stitches. *Using the point of the left-hand needle, lift the first stitch on the right-hand needle over the second then drop it off the needle. Knit the next stitch and repeat from * until all stitches have been worked off the left-hand needle and only one stitch remains on the right-hand needle. Cut the yarn (leaving enough to sew in the end), thread the end through the stitch then slip it off the needle. Draw the yarn up firmly to fasten off.

Purlwise

Purl two stitches. *Using the point of the left-hand needle, lift the first stitch on the right-hand needle over the second and drop it off the needle. Purl the next stitch and repeat from * until all the stitches have been worked off the left-hand needle and only one stitch remains on the right-hand

needle. Secure the last stitch as described for binding off knitwise.

The excitement of arriving at the last stage of your knitting can make you bind off without the same care that you have used in the rest of the work. You should take into account the part of the garment you are working on. If it is a neckband, you need to make sure that your bind-off edge is not too tight, preventing the neck from going over the wearer's head. If you are a tight knitter, you may need to bind off with a larger needle. Most neckbands or frontbands on a jacket or cardigan are worked in rib and should be bound off "ribwise" by knitting the knit stitches and purling the purl stitches as you bind off along the row. Lace stitches should also be bound off in pattern, slipping, making stitches, or decreasing as you go to make sure that the fabric doesn't widen or gather up.

Gauge (or tension)

The correct gauge (or tension) is the most important contribution to the successful knitting of a garment. The information under this heading given at the beginning of all patterns refers to the number of stitches required to fill a particular area; for example, a frequent gauge indication would be "22 sts and 30 rows = 4in (10cm) square measured over stockinette stitch on size 6 (4mm) needles." This means that it is necessary to produce fabric made up of the proportion of stitches and rows as given in the gauge paragraph in order to obtain the correct measurements for the garment you intend to knit, regardless of the needles you use. The needle size indicated in the pattern is the one which most knitters will use to achieve this gauge, but it is the gauge that is important, not needle size.

The way to ensure that you do achieve the correct gauge is to work a gauge sample or swatch before starting the main part of the knitting. Although this may seem to be time wasting and a nuisance, it can save the enormous amount of time and aggravation that would result from having knitted a garment the wrong size.

Gauge Swatch

The instructions given in the gauge paragraph of a knitting pattern are either for working in stockinette stitch or in pattern stitch. If they are given in pattern stitch, it is necessary to work a multiple of stitches the same as the multiple required in the pattern. If in stockinette stitch, any number can be cast on, but whichever method is used there should always be at least 5in (13cm) wide. Work in pattern or stockinette stitch according to the wording of the gauge paragraph until the piece measures at least 4in (10cm) in depth. Break the yarn about 6in (15cm) from the work and thread this end through the stitches, then remove the

knitting needle. Place a pin vertically into the fabric a few stitches from the side edge. Measure 4in (10cm) carefully and insert a second pin. Count the stitches. If the number of stitches between the pins is fewer than specified in the pattern (even by half a stitch) your garment will be too large. Use smaller needles and knit another gauge sample. If your sample has more stitches over 4in (10cm), the garment will be too small. Change to larger needles. Check the number of rows against the given gauge also.

It is most important to get the width measurement correct before starting to knit. Length measurements can usually be adjusted during the course of the knitting by adjusting the measurements to underarm or sleeve length, which is frequently given as a measurement and not in rows.

Following Charts

You should read a chart in the same way as you proceed with a piece of knitting: working from the bottom to the top. Each colored block on the chart represents a stitch and each horizontal line a row (or part of a row, if the pattern is to be repeated across the whole width of the knitted piece).

Before starting to knit, take a good look at the chart to familiarize yourself with the pattern. When you have the right side of your work facing you, you need to follow the chart from right to left; when working on the reverse (wrong side), follow the chart from left to right. As you proceed, it may help you to keep track of where you are on the chart by placing a ruler above the line you are working.

Right-side rows are those where the right side of the fabric is facing you when you work, and wrong-side rows are those where the wrong side is facing you when you work. Row numbers are shown at the side of each chart, at the beginning of the row.

Pattern Repeats and Multiples

The "multiple" or repeat of a pattern is given with each chart. For example, "multiple of 6" means that you can cast on any number of stitches which is divisible by 6. This multiple is then repeated across the row the required number of times. In some charts, the pattern repeat is contained between heavier vertical lines. In some cases, there may be extra stitches at either end of a pattern repeat, which are edge stitches worked at the beginning and end of rows to complete the pattern and make the overall design symmetrical.

The simplest form of Fair Isle knitting is to repeat a single pattern over the entire width and depth of the fabric. A pattern band repeated many times becomes an all-over pattern; interesting effects can be also achieved by combining different pattern bands. As a general rule, it is best, when combining patterns, to choose those that have a similar number of stitches in their repeat.

As well as being repeated along the row, the number of rows in a pattern is also taken into consideration. Bands of patterns can vary from as little as one single row to 30 or more rows. Narrow bands, or "peeries" have between one and seven rows and are generally used to separate larger bands. Border patterns are those with between 9 and 15 rows and are perfect for edgings or for all-over pattern repeats. Larger borders, with more than 15 rows, are generally based on "OXO" designs—in other words, diamonds and crosses.

You will also see that there are a number of single star and snowflake motifs in this book. Like any of the other patterns, these can be repeated across a piece of knitted fabric; once again, take note of the number denoting the multiple or repeat, which is given with each chart.

stitch gallery

Little Dots (single)

Rep 2 sts × I row

Little Dots (double)

Rep 3 sts × I row

Short Dash

Rep 3 sts × 1 row

Dash

Rep 4 sts × 1 row

Dot and Dash

Rep 5 sts × 1 row

Long Dash

Rep 6 sts × 1 row

Dot and Long Dash

Rep 6 sts x 1 row

Small Zigzag

Rep 2 sts x 2 rows

Small Wave

1

Rep 3 sts × 2 rows

Back Stroke

1

Rep 4 sts × 2 rows

Two-Wave

Rep 4 sts × 2 rows

Three-Wave

Rep 6 sts × 2 rows

Small Arch

Rep 8 sts x 2 rows

Triangle Wave I

Rep 6 sts x 2 rows

Seeded Vertical Stripe

1

Rep 6 sts × 2 rows

Triangle and Square I

Rep 14 sts × 2 rows

Threaded Squares

Rep 6 sts × 3 rows

Triangle and Square II

3
1

Rep 14 sts x 4 rows

Tall Blocks

Rep 3 sts x 3 rows

Post and Hook

Rep 3 sts × 3 rows

Broken Fence

Rep 4 sts × 3 rows

Single Fence

Rep 4 sts × 3 rows

Broken Rows I

Rep 4 sts x 3 rows

Broken Rows II

Rep 8 sts × 3 rows

Small Arrowhead

Rep 3 sts × 3 rows

Speckled Fence

Rep 4 sts × 3 rows

High Tide

3

1

Rep 6 sts × 3 rows

Kirkwall Border

Rep 6 sts x 4 rows

Dancing Bears

Rep 4 sts x 2 rows

Triangle Stacks

Rep 12 sts × 3 rows

Flotsam

5

3

1

Rep 12 sts x 6 rows

Battlements (3-count)

Rep 4 sts x 3 rows

Breakers

Rep 5 sts × 3 rows

Battlements (4-count) I

3

1

Rep 6 sts x 3 rows

Battlements (4-count) II

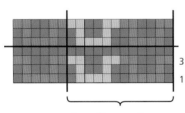

3
1

Rep 12 sts x 4 rows

Heather Peerie

3

1

Rep 6 sts x 4 rows

Triangle and Dot

3

1

Rep 6 sts × 3 rows

Shoots and Seeds

3

1

Rep 10 sts x 3 rows

Triangle Wave II

5

3

1

Rep 6 sts x 6 rows

Outline Triangle

Rep 6 sts x 4 rows

Five and One

Rep 6 sts x 3 rows

Harvest Furrows

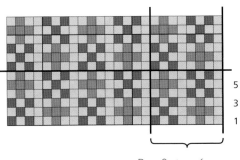

5
3
1

Rep 8 sts x 6 rows

Triangle Wave III

3

1

Rep 6 sts x 3 rows

Triangle Wave Border

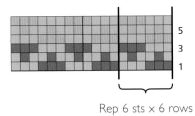

5
3
1

Rep 6 sts x 6 rows

H-border

Rep 4 sts x 3 rows

Ploughed Furrows

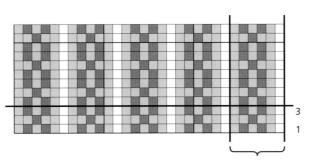

3
1

Rep 6 sts x 3 rows

Triangles and Strokes

Rep 16 sts x 3 rows

Tree of Life

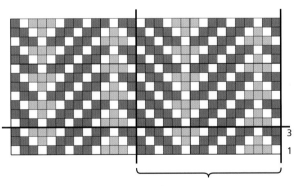

3

1

Rep 16 sts × 3 rows

Diagonal Lattice

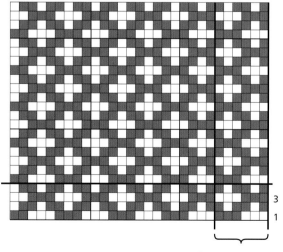

3

1

Rep 6 sts × 4 rows

Seeded Back Stroke

3

1

Rep 5 sts × 3 rows

Box and Dot

3

1

Rep 6 sts × 3 rows

Chequered Dot Border

5

3

1

Rep 6 sts x 6 rows

Gull Wings

Rep 12 sts x 4 rows

Twinkling Diamonds

5
3
1

Rep 6 sts × 5 rows

Broken Crests

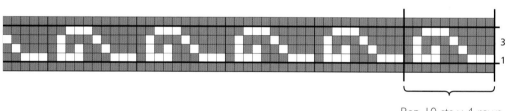

3

1

Rep 10 sts × 4 rows

Rocky Shore

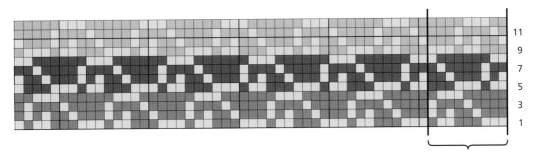

Rep 9 sts × 12 rows

11
9
7
5
3
1

Broken Zigzags

3

1

Rep 6 sts x 4 rows

Battlements (5-count)

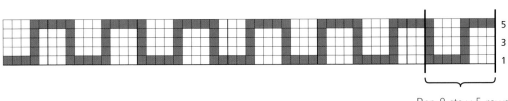

5
3
1

Rep 8 sts x 5 rows

Stormy Sea

Rep 20 sts × 5 rows

Arrowhead Tweed Border

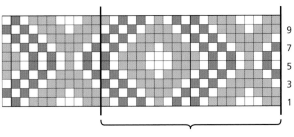

Rep 20 sts × 10 rows

Bannock Trellis Pattern

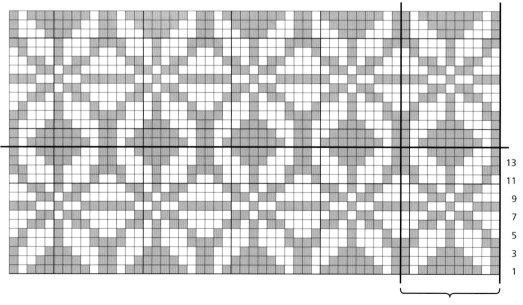

13
11
9
7
5
3
1

Rep 11 sts x 19 rows

Tulip Wave

3

1

Rep 14 sts x 4 rows

Wave Crest I

Rep 6 sts × 5 rows

Wave Crest II

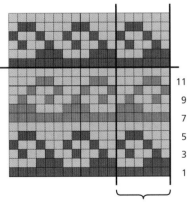

11
9
7
5
3
1

Rep 6 sts × 12 rows

Lattice Window I

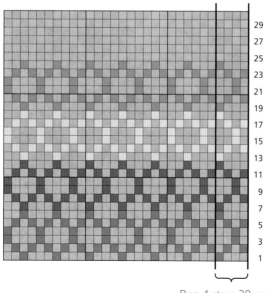

29
27
25
23
21
19
17
15
13
11
9
7
5
3
1

Rep 4 sts × 30 rows

Flight

Rep 8 sts × 6 rows

Triangle Zigzag

5
3
1

Rep 6 sts × 5 rows

Pretty Maids

Rep 6 sts × 5 rows

Crossed Battlements

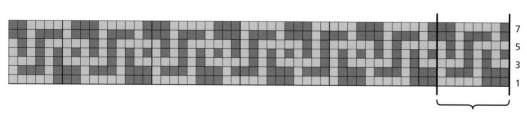

7
5
3
1

Rep 8 sts x 7 rows

Phlox

Rep 6 sts x 7 rows

Double-row Diamond

Rep 4 sts x 6 rows

Diamond Footpath

5
3
1

Rep 4 sts x 6 rows

Rose and Thistle

Rep 10 sts × 5 rows

Diamond Tweed Pattern

7
5
3
1

Rep 8 sts × 7 rows

Wave and Diamond Border

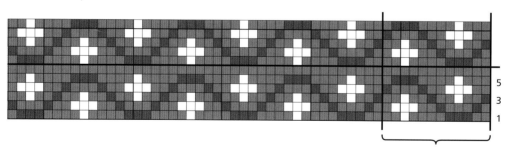

5
3
1

Rep 12 sts x 6 rows

Celtic Rose

5
3
1

Rep 8 sts x 5 rows

Diamond Link and Dot

Rep 6 sts × 7 rows

Speckled Trellis

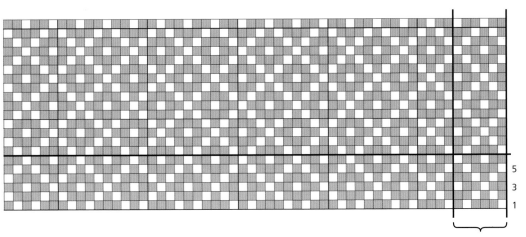

5
3
1

Rep 6 sts × 6 rows

Captive Diamond Border

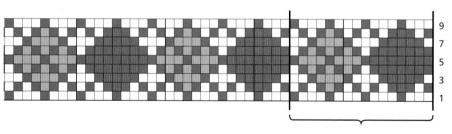

Rep 16 sts x 18 rows

Zigzag Fence

Rep 8 sts × 7 rows

Diamond Filigree

Rep 8 sts x 5 rows

Cabbages

Rep 8 sts x 5 rows

Diamond Box Border

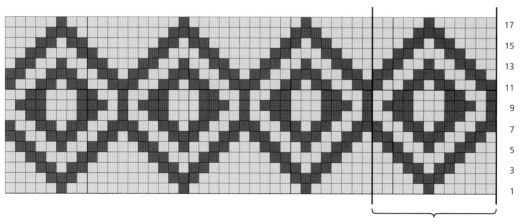

Rep 12 sts x 17 rows

Wandering Zigzag

Rep 10 sts x 7 rows

Diamond and Cross Windowpane

Rep 12 sts x 9 rows

Flower and Chalice

Rep 9 sts x 8 rows

Wall-walk

Rep 5 sts x 6 rows

Lattice Window II

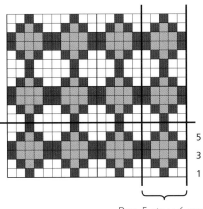

5
3
1

Rep 5 sts x 6 rows

Diamond and Cross

Rep 10 sts x 5 rows

Trellis with Blocks

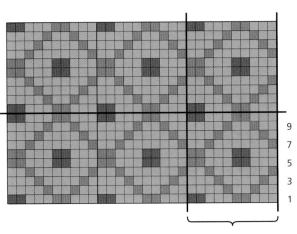

Rep 10 sts x 10 rows

Speckled Zigzag

Rep 6 sts x 6 rows

Zigzag Tweed

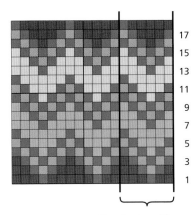

17
15
13
11
9
7
5
3
1

Rep 6 sts x 18 rows

Aubrieta

Rep 6 sts × 13 rows

Vertical Basketweave Lattice

Rep 30 sts × 8 rows

Arrowhead Zigzag

Rep 16 sts x 9 rows

Ripples Border

Rep 5 sts x 9 rows

Cosmea

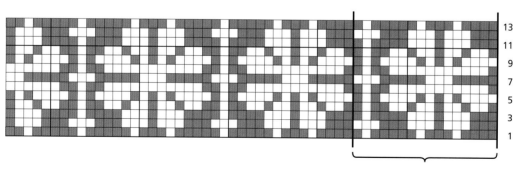

Rep 16 sts × 13 rows

Diamond and Cross Windowpane II

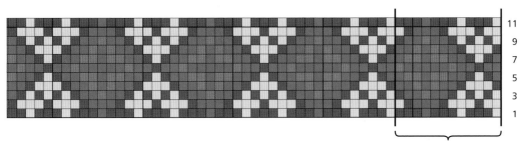

11
9
7
5
3
1

Rep 12 sts x 11 rows

Mosaic Path

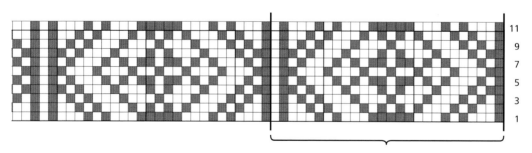

Rep 26 sts x 11 rows

Castle Window I

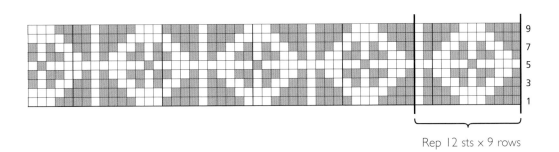

9
7
5
3
1

Rep 12 sts x 9 rows

Castle Window II

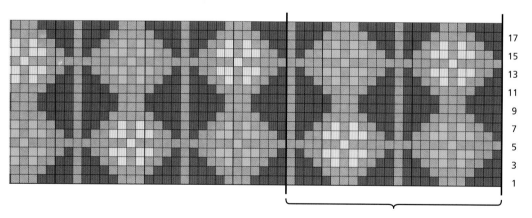

Rep 24 sts x 18 rows

17
15
13
11
9
7
5
3
1

Flora

5

3

1

Rep 6 sts x 6 rows

Vertical Stripe I

Rep 2 sts x 1 row

Line and Dot I

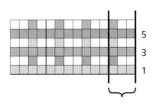

5

3

1

Rep 2 sts × 6 rows

Diamond Links

5

3

1

Rep 4 sts x 5 rows

Vertical Stripes II

Rep 3 sts × 1 row

Country Lanes

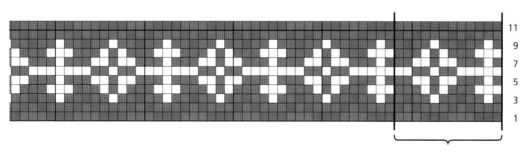

Rep 12 sts x 11 rows

Line and Dot II

5
3
1

Rep 2 sts x 6 rows

Double Verticle Stripes

Rep 4 sts x 1 row

Chain Link I

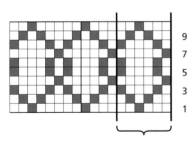

9
7
5
3
1

Rep 6 sts × 10 rows

Chain Link II

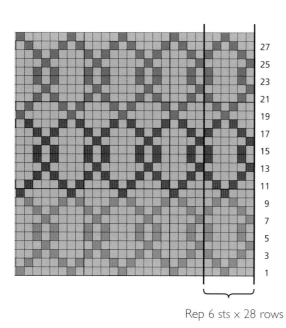

27
25
23
21
19
17
15
13
11
9
7
5
3
1

Rep 6 sts × 28 rows

Melissa

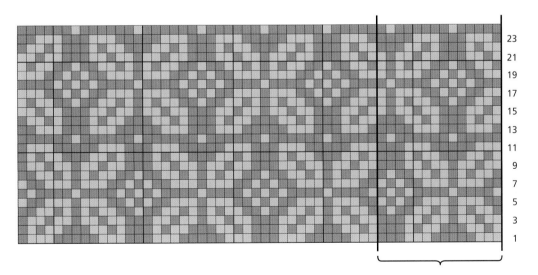

23
21
19
17
15
13
11
9
7
5
3
1

Rep 14 sts × 24 rows

Diamonds in the Snow

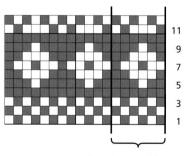

11
9
7
5
3
1

Rep 6 sts × 12 rows

Shuttered Windows

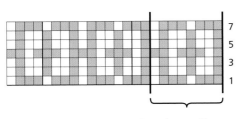

7
5
3
1

Rep 8 sts x 7 rows

Kirkwall

Rep 8 sts x 16 rows

Argyll Check

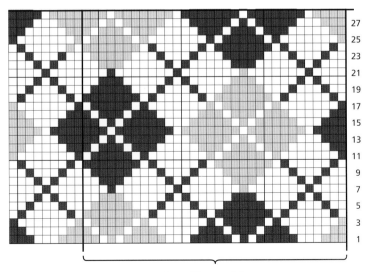

Rep 32 sts x 28 rows

													27
													25
													23
													21
													19
													17
													15
													13
													11
													9
													7
													5
													3
													1

Diamond Zigzag Bands

11
9
7
5
3
1

Rep 6 sts × 12 rows

Crossroads

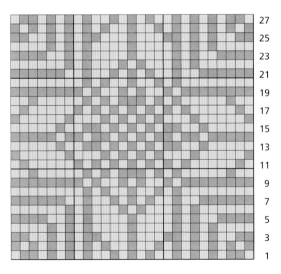

Rep 27 sts × 27 rows

Parterre

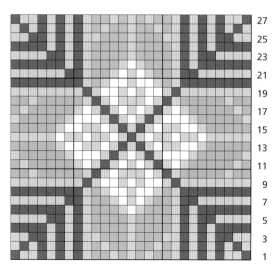

27
25
23
21
19
17
15
13
11
9
7
5
3
1

Rep 27 sts x 27 rows

Ladder of Hope

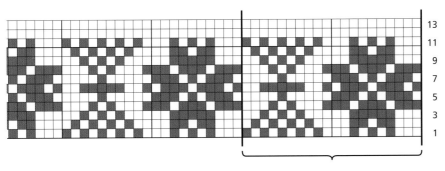

Rep 20 sts x 13 rows

Harbour Walls Motif

Rep 24 sts × 24 rows

Berwick

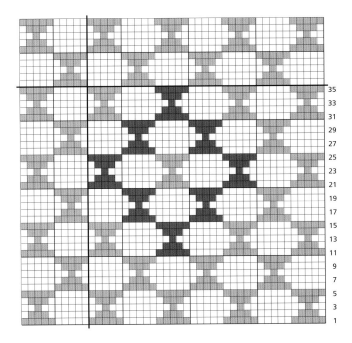

35
33
31
29
27
25
23
21
19
17
15
13
11
9
7
5
3
1

Rep 35 sts × 35 rows

Speckled Pinnacles

Rep 12 sts x 9 rows

Broken Zigzag Rows

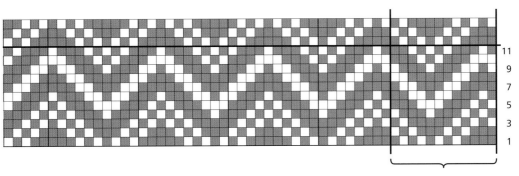

11
9
7
5
3
1

Rep 12 sts x 11 rows

Large Chain Link

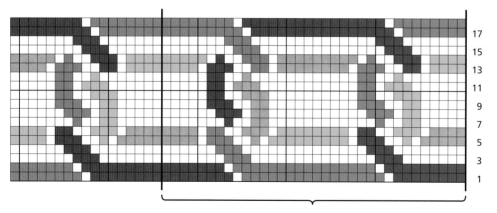

Rep 34 sts x 18 rows

Sprigged Snowflake Medallion

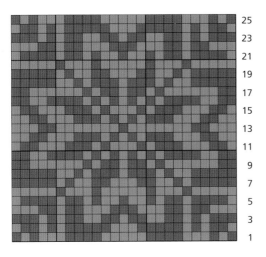

Rep 25 sts × 25 rows

Lattice Heart Border

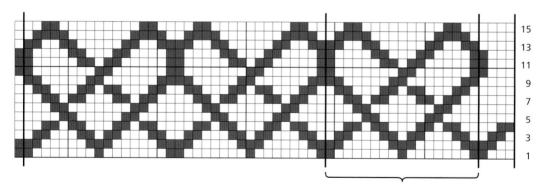

Rep 17 sts x 15 rows

15
13
11
9
7
5
3
1

Fish Hooks

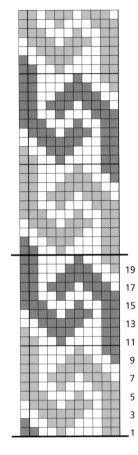

19
17
15
13
11
9
7
5
3
1

Rep 11 sts × 20 rows

Gallery Motif

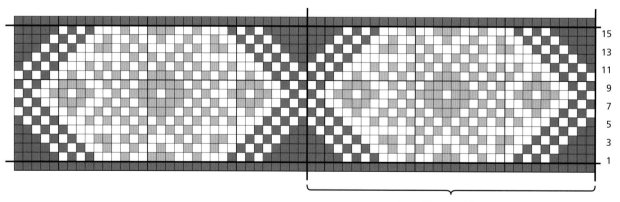

15
13
11
9
7
5
3
1

Rep 32 sts x 15 rows

Lillestrom Panel

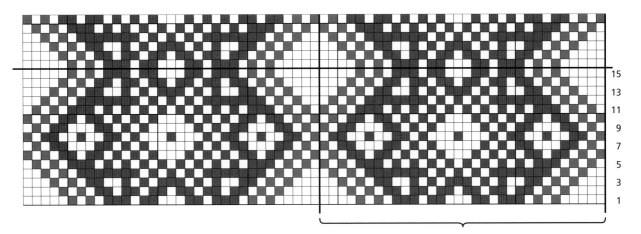

Rep 32 sts x 15 rows

Oslo Snowflake Motif

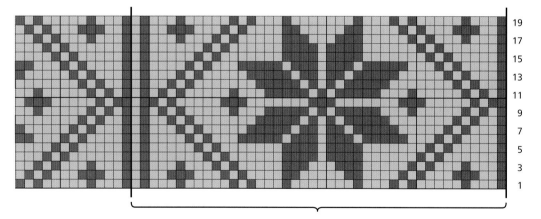

Rep 42 sts x 19 rows

Star and Arrow Lattice

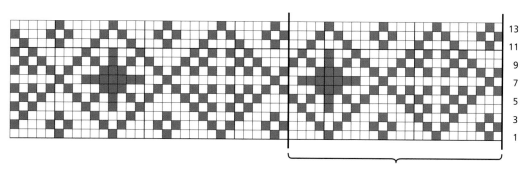

Rep 24 sts x 13 rows

Banded Lattice and Cross

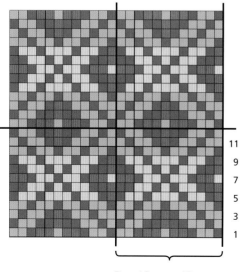

11
9
7
5
3
1

Rep 12 sts x 12 rows

Heraldic Border

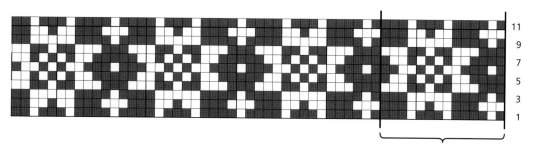

Rep 14 sts x 11 rows

Flotilla

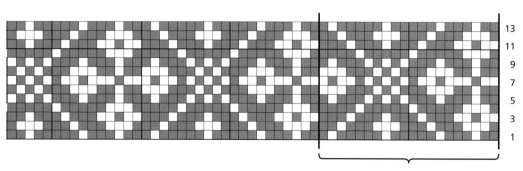

Rep 20 sts x 13 rows

Trondheim Border

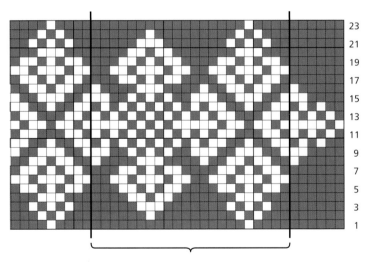

											23
											21
											19
											17
											15
											13
											11
											9
											7
											5
											3
											1

Rep 22 sts x 23 rows

Quadrant Cross

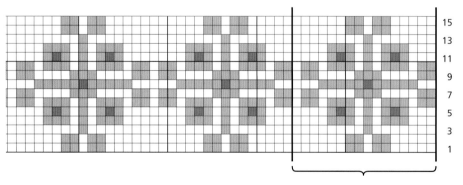

Rep 16 sts x 15 rows

North Cape I

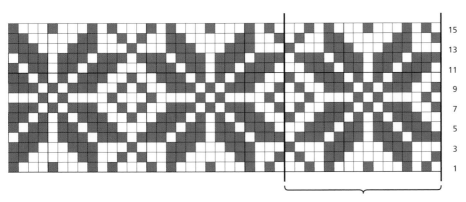

Rep 16 sts x 15 rows

North Cape II

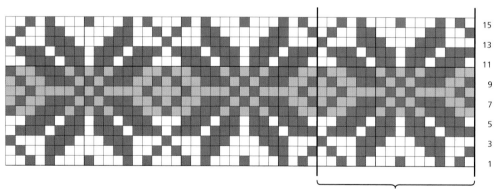

Rep 16 sts x 15 rows

Speckled Snowflake Medallion

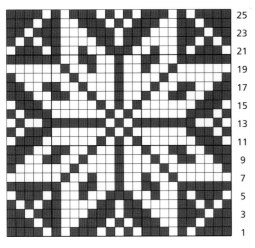

25
23
21
19
17
15
13
11
9
7
5
3
1

Rep 25 sts x 25 rows

Solid Snowflake

Rep 25 sts × 25 rows

Claymore

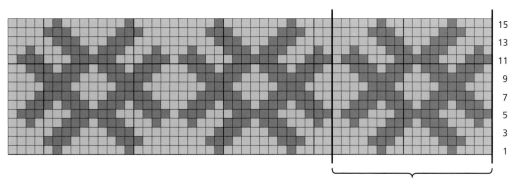

Rep 18 sts x 15 rows

Ship in Full Sail

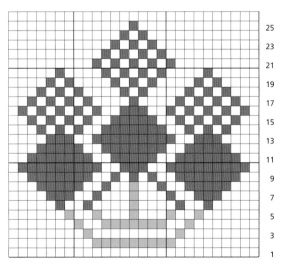

Rep 27 sts x 26 rows

Minerva

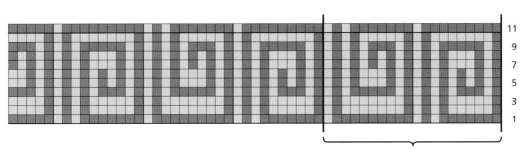

11
9
7
5
3
1

Rep 20 sts × 11 rows

Two Tribes

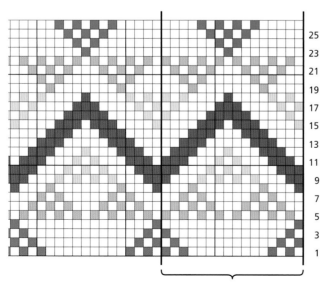

	25
	23
	21
	19
	17
	15
	13
	11
	9
	7
	5
	3
	1

Rep 16 sts x 26 rows

Tromso Snowflake

Rep 31 sts × 31 rows

St Nicholas Snowflake

Rep 31 sts x 31 rows

Norland Snowflake

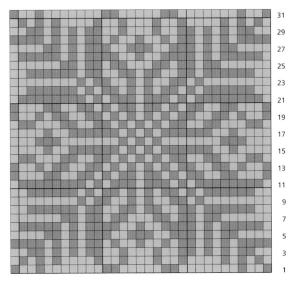

Rep 31 sts × 31 rows

Avenue

15
13
11
9
7
5
3
1

Rep 10 sts × 16 rows

Jacobean Flower Border

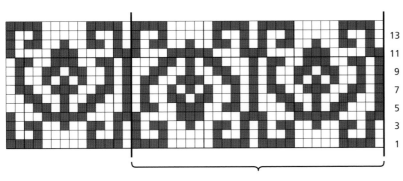

13
11
9
7
5
3
1

Rep 28 sts x 14 rows

Thistle and Ribbon

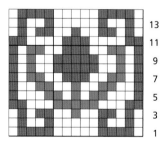

Rep 15 sts x 14 rows

Floret 1

	35
	33
	31
	29
	27
	25
	23
	21
	19
	17
	15
	13
	11
	9
	7
	5
	3
	1

Rep 33 sts × 35 rows

Floret 11

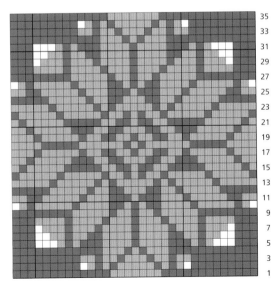

Rep 33 sts x 35 rows

Tromso Snowflake Panel

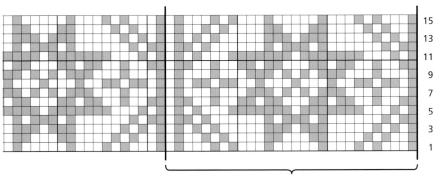

Rep 28 sts x 15 rows

Hydrangea Border

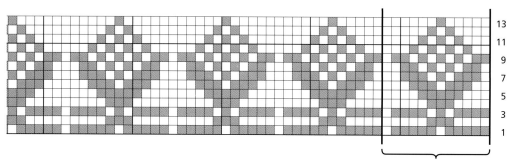

Rep 12 sts x 13 rows

Hydrangea Border II

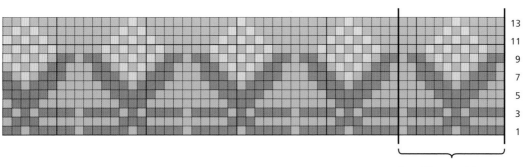

13
11
9
7
5
3
1

Rep 12 sts × 13 rows

Interlaced Tulips

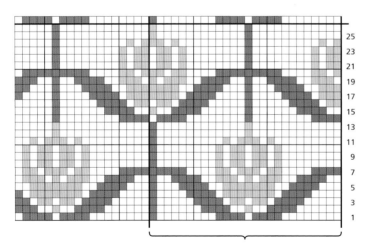

Rep 26 sts × 26 rows

Rambling Rose

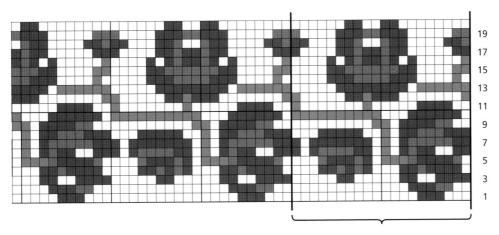

Rep 20 sts x 20 rows

Diamond Flower Border I

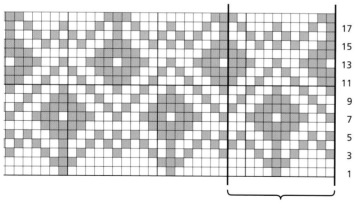

Rep 12 sts x 18 rows

Diamond Flower Border II

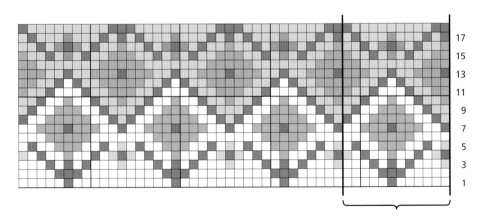

Rep 12 sts x 18 rows

											17	
											15	
											13	
											11	
											9	
											7	
											5	
											3	
											1	

Whirligig

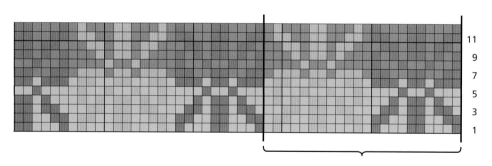

11
9
7
5
3
1

Rep 22 sts x 12 rows

Diamond and Snowflake Paths

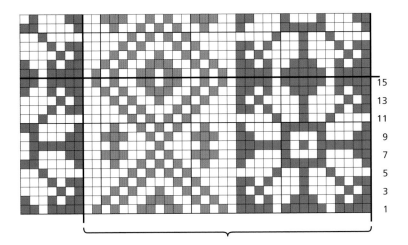

15
13
11
9
7
5
3
1

Rep 32 sts x 15 rows

Rose Crest

Rep 27 sts x 27 rows

Winter Rose Medallion

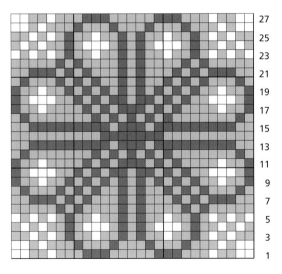

Rep 27 sts × 27 rows

Dancing Diamonds

Rep 8 sts x 25 rows

Multiple Stripes

Rep 1 st x 10 rows

Diamond and Lozenge Tweed Border

27
25
23
21
19
17
15
13
11
9
7
5
3
1

Rep 10 sts × 27 rows

Diamond and Lozenge Banded Border

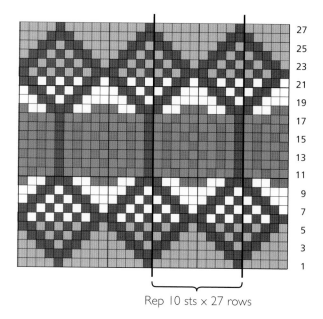

27
25
23
21
19
17
15
13
11
9
7
5
3
1

Rep 10 sts x 27 rows

Scottish Thistles I

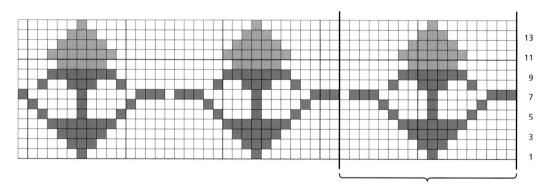

Rep 18 sts x 14 rows

Scottish Thistles II

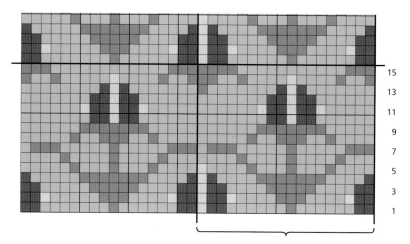

Rep 18 sts x 15 rows

15
13
11
9
7
5
3
1

Cairn

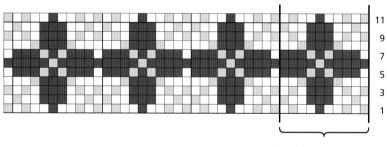

												11
												9
												7
												5
												3
												1

Rep 10 sts x 11 rows

Sheild and Cross

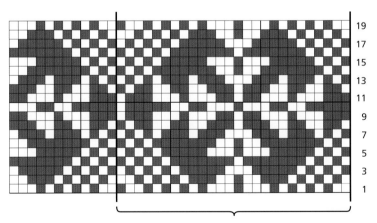

Rep 26 sts x 19 rows

Little Minch

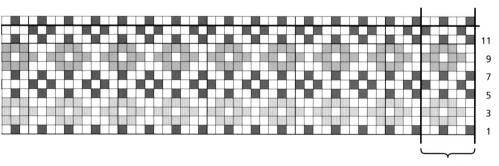

11
9
7
5
3
1

Rep 6 sts x 12 rows

Grandma's Garden

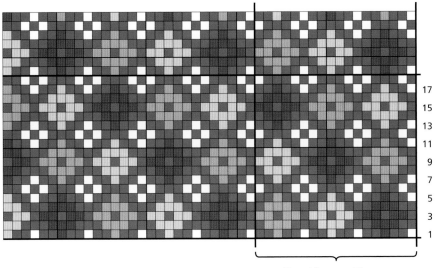

17
15
13
11
9
7
5
3
1

Rep 18 sts × 18 rows

Quatrefoil

Rep 27 sts x 27 rows

Argyll Diamond Motif

Rep 27 sts x 27 rows

Hellenic Wave

Rep 14 sts × 9 rows

Algorithm

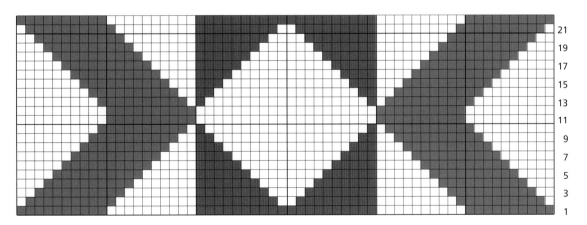

Rep 60 sts x 22 rows

Diathus and Pannier Border

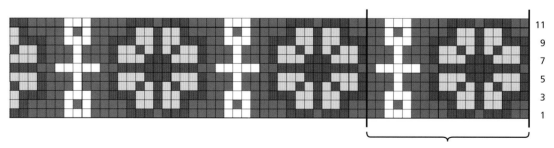

Rep 18 sts x 11 rows

11
9
7
5
3
1

Campion and Pannier Border

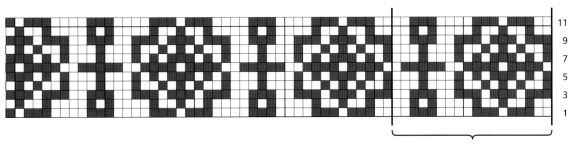

Rep 18 sts x 11 rows

Herbaceous Border

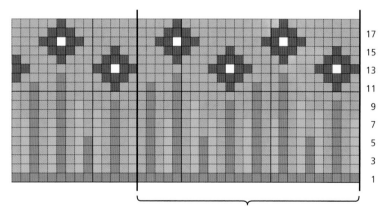

Rep 25 sts x 18 rows

Large Vertical Stripe

Rep 19 sts x 1 row

Even Stripes

Rep 1 st x 8 rows

Uneven Stripes

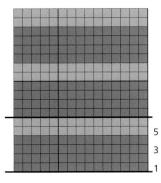

5
3
1

Rep 1 st x 6 rows

Michaelmas

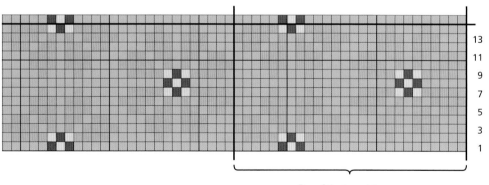

13
11
9
7
5
3
1

Rep 26 sts x 14 rows

Stepping Stones

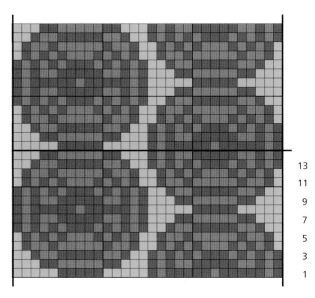

13
11
9
7
5
3
1

Rep 30 sts × 14 rows

Lads and Lasses I

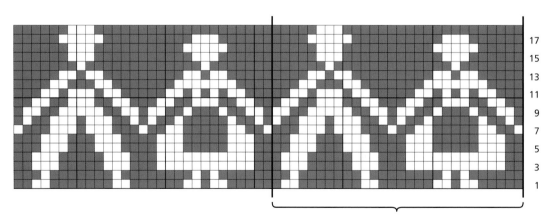

17
15
13
11
9
7
5
3
1

Rep 28 sts x 18 rows

Lads and Lasses II

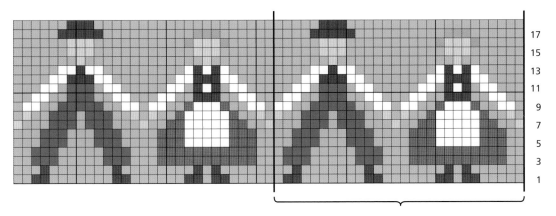

Rep 28 sts x 18 rows

Framed Heart Motif

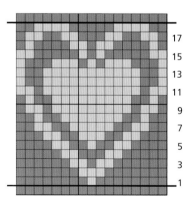

Rep 17 sts x 18 rows

Christmas Lights

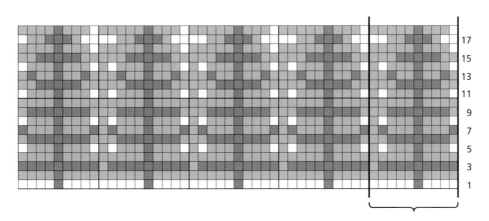

Rep 10 sts x 18 rows

Acrobats

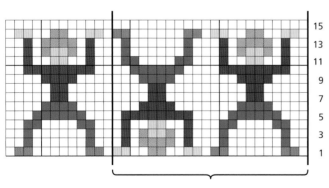

Rep 22 sts x 15 rows

Dancing Ballerinas

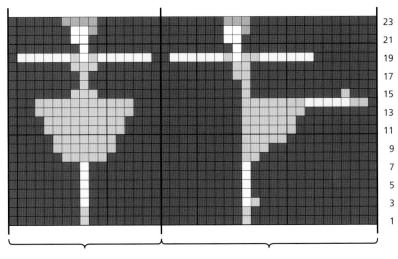

Rep 17 sts + 24 sts x 23 rows

23
21
19
17
15
13
11
9
7
5
3
1

Belladonna

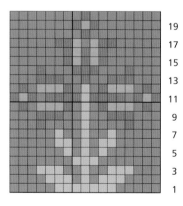

Rep 17 sts x 20 rows

Campion

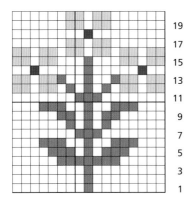

Rep 17sts x 20 rows

Standard Flower

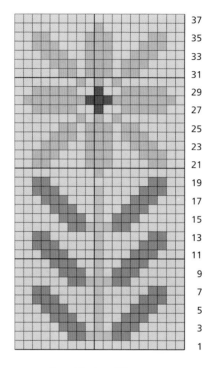

Rep 19 sts × 37 rows

Foxglove

Rep 19 sts x 37 rows

Juniper

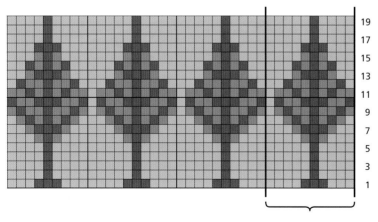

19
17
15
13
11
9
7
5
3
1

Rep 10 sts x 19 rows

Pansy Trio

Rep 26 sts × 35 rows

Solid Heart

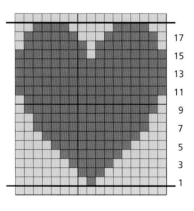

Rep 17 sts x 18 rows

Dancing Ladies

Rep 35 sts × 32 rows

Saxifrage

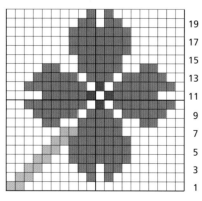

Rep 20 sts x 20 rows

Single Bud

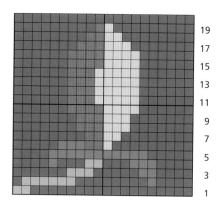

Rep 20 sts x 20 rows

Cranesbill

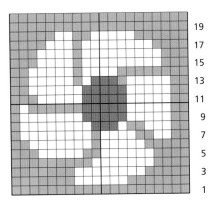

Rep 20 sts x 20 rows

Magnolia

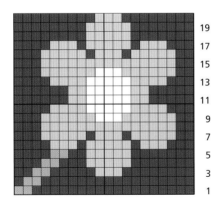

19
17
15
13
11
9
7
5
3
1

Rep 20 sts x 20 rows

Marching Reindeer

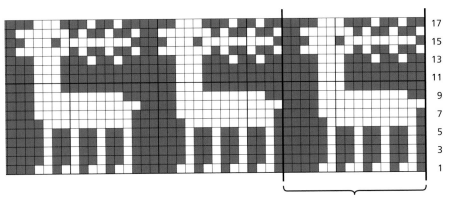

Rep 16 sts x 17 rows

Large Tulip

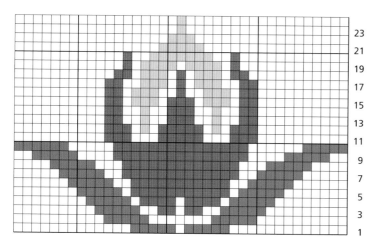

Rep 37 sts × 24 rows

Butterflies

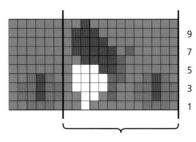

Rep 13 sts × 10 rows

Pig

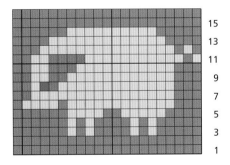

15
13
11
9
7
5
3
1

Rep 21 sts x 16 rows

Horse

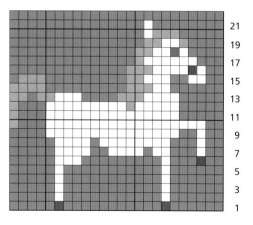

Rep 24 sts x 22 rows

Playful Kitten

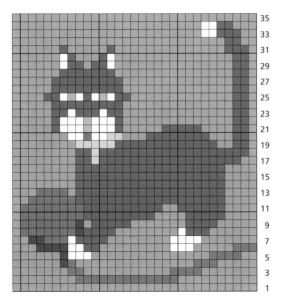

Rep 31 sts x 35 rows

Musical Notes

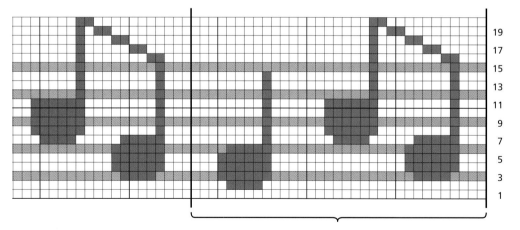

Rep 32 sts x 20 rows

Balloon

Rep 10 sts × 15 rows

Snowman

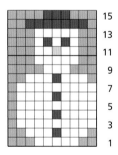

Rep 10 sts × 15 rows

Rocket

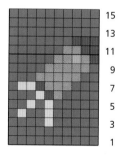

15
13
11
9
7
5
3
1

Rep 10 sts × 15 rows

Little House

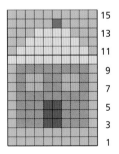

Rep 10 sts × 15 rows

Key

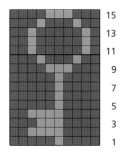

Rep 10 sts × 15 rows

Umbrella

Rep 10 sts × 15 rows

Anchor

Rep 10 sts × 15 rows

Rabbit

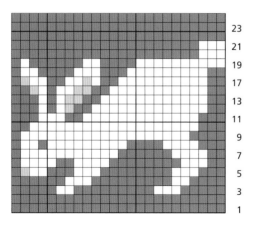

Rep 24 sts x 22 rows

A

B

Rep 8 sts × 12 rows

Rep 8 sts × 12 rows

C

_____

11							
								9
								7
								5
								3
								1

Rep 8 sts × 12 rows

D

_____

11							
								9
								7
								5
								3
								1

Rep 8 sts × 12 rows

E

F

Rep 8 sts × 12 rows

Rep 8 sts × 12 rows

G

H

Rep 8 sts × 12 rows

Rep 8 sts × 12 rows

I

J

Rep 8 sts × 12 rows

Rep 8 sts × 12 rows

K

L

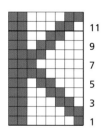

Rep 8 sts × 12 rows

Rep 8 sts × 12 rows

M

N

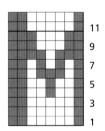

Rep 8 sts × 12 rows

Rep 8 sts × 12 rows

O

P

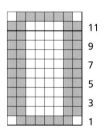

Rep 8 sts × 12 rows

Rep 8 sts × 12 rows

Q

Rep 8 sts × 12 rows

R

Rep 8 sts × 12 rows

S

Rep 8 sts × 12 rows

T

Rep 8 sts × 12 rows

U

Rep 8 sts × 12 rows

V

Rep 8 sts × 12 rows

W

X

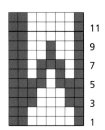

Rep 8 sts × 12 rows

Rep 8 sts × 12 rows

Y

Z

Rep 8 sts × 12 rows

Rep 8 sts × 12 rows

a

b

Rep 6 sts × 9 rows

Rep 6 sts × 9 rows

c

d

Rep 6 sts x 9 rows

Rep 6 sts x 9 rows

e

f

Rep 6 sts × 9 rows

Rep 6 sts × 9 rows

g

h

Rep 6 sts × 9 rows

Rep 6 sts × 9 rows

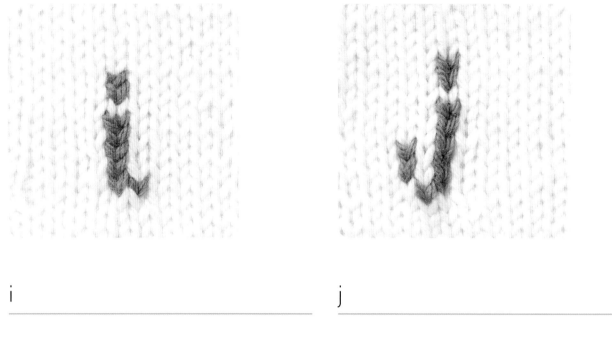

i

Rep 6 sts × 9 rows

j

Rep 6 sts × 9 rows

k

Rep 6 sts x 9 rows

l

Rep 6 sts x 9 rows

m

9
7
5
3
1

Rep 6 sts x 9 rows

n

9
7
5
3
1

Rep 6 sts x 9 rows

O

p

Rep 6 sts × 9 rows

Rep 6 sts × 9 rows

q

r

9
7
5
3
1

Rep 6 sts x 9 rows

9
7
5
3
1

Rep 6 sts x 9 rows

s

Rep 6 sts x 9 rows

t

Rep 6 sts x 9 rows

u

Rep 6 sts x 9 rows

V

Rep 6 sts x 9 rows

W

X

Rep 6 sts x 9 rows

Rep 6 sts x 9 rows

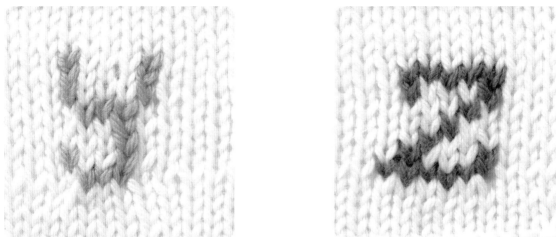

y

z

Rep 6 sts × 9 rows

Rep 6 sts × 9 rows

1

2

Rep 8 sts × 12 rows

Rep 8 sts × 12 rows

3

4

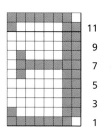

11
9
7
5
3
1

Rep 8 sts × 12 rows

11
9
7
5
3
1

Rep 8 sts × 12 rows

5

6

Rep 8 sts × 12 rows

Rep 8 sts × 12 rows

7

8

Rep 8 sts × 12 rows

Rep 8 sts × 12 rows

9

0

Rep 8 sts × 12 rows

Rep 8 sts × 12 rows

index

inspiring resources
from Interweave